WORLD'S STRANGEST

OCEAN BEASTS

Produced for Lonely Planet by Plum5 Limited
Authors: Stuart Derrick & Charlotte Goddard
Editor: Plum5 Limited
Designer: Plum5 Limited
Publishing Director: Piers Pickard
Art Director: Andy Mansfield
Commissioning Editors: Catharine Robertson, Jen Feroze
Assistant Editor: Christina Webb
Print Production: Nigel Longuet, Lisa Ford
With thanks to: Jennifer Dixon

Published in August 2018 by Lonely Planet Global Ltd

CRN: 554153
ISBN: 978 1 78701 302 5

www.lonelyplanetkids.com
© Lonely Planet 2018

Printed in China
2 4 6 8 10 9 7 5 3 1

STAY IN TOUCH – lonelyplanet.com/contact
Lonely Planet Offices
AUSTRALIA The Malt Store, Level 3, 551 Swanston St, Carlton,
Victoria 3053 T: 03 8379 8000
IRELAND Digital Depot, Roe Lane (off Thomas St),
Digital Hub, Dublin 8, D08 TCV4
USA 124 Linden St, Oakland, CA 94607 T: 510 250 6400
UK 240 Blackfriars Rd, London SE1 8NW T: 020 3771 5100

WORLD'S STRANGEST

OCEAN BEASTS

Stuart Derrick &
Charlotte Goddard

PICTURE CREDITS

CONTENTS

INTRODUCTION

More than 70 percent of our planet is covered in seawater, and our oceans contain millions of amazing creatures. Join us to find out about the most fascinating and creepy creatures, and learn which is the weirdest of them all.

We've ranked the world's strangest ocean beasts to find out about...

⭐ Their crazy skills

⭐ Their bizarre habits

⭐ Their jaw-dropping looks

In this book, you're about to meet:

⭐ The biggest animal that the world has ever known

⭐ A creature with eyes on the end of its arms

⭐ A color-changing master of disguise

⭐ A fish wearing lipstick

⭐ The fashion designer of the sea

... and many more!

STRANGEOMETER

The creatures in this book are all unique in their own ways, so we've used a special strangeometer to rank them. This is made up of four categories with a score out of 25 for each.

These categories are...

STRANGEOMETER

APPEARANCE		17/25
WEIRD ABILITIES		8/25
RARITY		12/25
STRANGENESS		13/25
STRANGEOMETER SCORE		50/100

APPEARANCE
This considers how stunning the ocean creature looks.

WEIRD ABILITIES
What unusual skills does the creature have that make it stand out from the crowd?

RARITY
How likely are you to encounter this creature? Some are very rare indeed!

STRANGENESS
What is the "wow factor" for this underwater creature?

STRANGEOMETER SCORE
These are added up to get a strangeometer score out of 100!

#40

The basking shark is covered in a very smelly slime that can rot fishing nets.

Although it usually swims slowly, this shark can jump completely out of the water, probably to try to get rid of parasites on its skin.

BASKING SHARK

The big-mouthed basking shark is the second-biggest fish in the seas. However, it survives by eating some of the ocean's smallest creatures: plankton.

I CAN FILTER 2,000 TONS OF SEAWATER AN HOUR. GULP!

Coastal Arctic and temperate waters

STRANGEOMETER

APPEARANCE		12/25
WEIRD ABILITIES		11/25
RARITY		12/25
STRANGENESS		11/25
STRANGEOMETER SCORE		46/100

TRUMPETFISH

These fish often swim vertically with their heads pointing downward, trying to blend in with coral. They also disguise themselves as floating sticks to surprise the small reef fish that they eat.

STRANGEOMETER

🐟 APPEARANCE	14/25
⚡ WEIRD ABILITIES	14/25
❓ RARITY	4/25
👁 STRANGENESS	15/25
⭐ STRANGEOMETER SCORE	47/100

The clever trumpetfish can change color to look like its prey. This allows it to get really close before grabbing its dinner.

CAN I STICK
WITH YOU?

trumpetfish
often hitch a ride
with larger fish,
swimming beside
them to sneak up
on prey or protect
themselves from
predators.

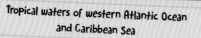

Tropical waters of western Atlantic Ocean
and Caribbean Sea

#38

Some sea pens can grow up to 6.5 ft. (2 m) tall, but most are smaller than that.

Most sea pens glow when they are touched.

CAN I BE YOUR PEN PAL?

Worldwide

A sea pen is not actually one animal but a whole group of tiny animals called polyps.

STRANGEOMETER

APPEARANCE		18/25
WEIRD ABILITIES		13/25
RARITY		2/25
STRANGENESS		15/25
STRANGEOMETER SCORE		48/100

SEA PEN

Sea pens look like old-fashioned quill pens sticking out of the seabed.

SEA CUCUMBER

Tropical and temperate waters worldwide

When they think they are going to be attacked, some sea cucumbers spurt out sticky threads to trap their enemies.

There are around 1,250 kinds of sea cucumber. Despite the name, many of them don't really look like the cucumbers we eat. They can be covered in spikes, spots, or warts. They move about in herds.

DID SOMEONE MENTION SEAFOOD SALAD?

Sea cucumbers can throw their guts out of their body to distract predators, giving them time to escape. Their missing body parts grow back later!

STRANGEOMETER

APPEARANCE		13/25
WEIRD ABILITIES		18/25
RARITY		3/25
STRANGENESS		15/25
STRANGEOMETER SCORE		49/100

Like many corals, wire coral comes in lots of different colors — from yellow and red to blue and green.

I'M A BIT TIED UP AT THE MOMENT.

Tropical and subtropical seas

WIRE CORAL

As the name of this beautiful form of coral suggests, wire coral can be found in long strands or coils floating in tropical and subtropical seas.

STRANGEOMETER

🐟	APPEARANCE	17/25
⚡	WEIRD ABILITIES	8/25
❓	RARITY	12/25
👁	STRANGENESS	13/25
⭐	STRANGEOMETER SCORE	50/100

They can grow to more than 9 ft. (3 m) in length.

Many tiny creatures such as shrimp make their homes on wire coral.

#35

South Pacific and Indian Oceans

GIANT CLAM

Giant clams can be more than 3.3 ft. (1 m) in size and weigh more than 440 lb. (200 kg). They are the largest mollusks on Earth.

STRANGEOMETER

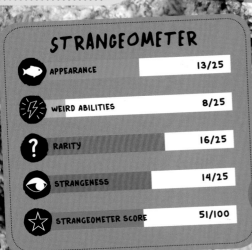

🐟 APPEARANCE		13/25
⚡ WEIRD ABILITIES		8/25
❓ RARITY		16/25
👁 STRANGENESS		14/25
⭐ STRANGEOMETER SCORE		51/100

I CAN LIVE FOR MORE THAN 100 YEARS.

Clams can make pearls, and the pearls are huge, too. The biggest one ever found weighed 75 lb. (34 kg). It was found by a fisherman in the Philippines, who kept it under his bed because he didn't know that it was worth up to $103 million!

COMB JELLY

The rows of hairs that line the sides of see-through comb jellies act as tiny oars, pushing them throught he water.

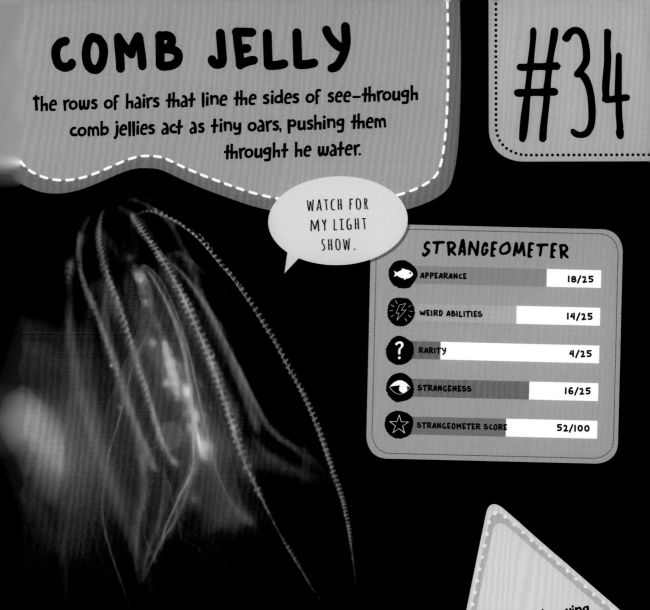

#34

WATCH FOR MY LIGHT SHOW.

STRANGEOMETER

APPEARANCE		18/25
WEIRD ABILITIES		14/25
RARITY		4/25
STRANGENESS		16/25
STRANGEOMETER SCORE		52/100

The jellies' moving hairs scatter light through the water and make the creatures look like they are covered in rainbows.

Comb jellies are ancient creatures that have roamed the seas for at least 500 million years. They use a sort of glue to stick their prey to their tentacles, before bringing the unlucky victim to their mouth and eating it.

Worldwide

#33

Ocean sunfish can grow as big as a car. They spend half the day sunbathing, which is how they got their name.

When a sunfish has too many parasites living on its skin, it pays a visit to a seagull. The gull pecks them off, leaving the sunfish nice and clean.

STRANGEOMETER

🐟	APPEARANCE	14/25
⚡	WEIRD ABILITIES	12/25
❓	RARITY	12/25
👁	STRANGENESS	15/25
⭐	STRANGEOMETER SCORE	53/100

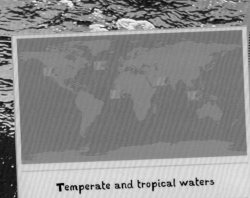

Temperate and tropical waters

MAKE SURE YOU PHOTOGRAPH MY BEST SIDE.

OCEAN SUNFISH

Sunfish produce more eggs than any other vertebrate – up to 300 million at a time.

#32

STRANGEOMETER

APPEARANCE		17/25
WEIRD ABILITIES		16/25
RARITY		3/25
STRANGENESS		18/25
STRANGEOMETER SCORE		54/100

Seahorses have no teeth or stomachs. They suck up food through their snouts like a vacuum cleaner. Baby seahorses eat an amazing 3,000 pieces of food a day!

Male and female seahorses pair for life. Every morning, the couple meets up and dances together for up to an hour.

SHALL WE DANCE?

SEAHORSE

Seahorse males give birth to the babies. The female lays eggs in a pocket-like pouch on the male's body, and two to six weeks later, baby seahorses are born.

Tropical waters around the world

I'M VERY TASTY – BUT DON'T TELL ANYBODY!

Caribbean Sea, North Atlantic and Indo-Pacific Oceans

STRANGEOMETER

APPEARANCE		15/25
WEIRD ABILITIES		15/25
RARITY		12/25
STRANGENESS		13/25
STRANGEOMETER SCORE		55/100

RED
LIONFISH

A lionfish can deliver venom through up to 18 needle-like fins. Its sting is extremely painful to humans but doesn't usually kill them.

Lionfish are invading seas around the United States and Europe, taking over from the fish that already live there. In the US, people are being encouraged to eat lionfish to get rid of them!

Lionfish sometimes spread their fins and herd small fish into tight corners so they can eat them more easily.

QUIZ

3. What do most sea pens do when touched?

How many types of sea cucumber are there?

4.

1. What is this fish?

How does the trumpetfish sneak up on its prey?

2.

6.

How long have comb jellies been on Earth?

What is this mollusk?

8.

7.

How many eggs does a sunfish produce?

5.

How long can wire coral grow?

What do male and female seahorses do every morning?

9.

10.

What can a lionfish do with its needle-like fins?

ANSWERS

1. A BASKING SHARK 2. IT CHANGES COLOR TO LOOK LIKE THE PREY
3. THEY GLOW 4. 1,250 5. MORE THAN 9 FT. (3 M) 6. A GIANT CLAM
7. 500 MILLION YEARS 8. 300 MILLION 9. DANCE 10. IT CAN STING YOU
WITH ITS VENOM

Caribbean, Gulf of Mexico, Amazon basin, West Africa

These gentle mammals are also called sea cows and are found in coastal waters and rivers. They feed on grass, algae, and weeds.

Manatees "walk" on the seafloor or riverbed with their flippers.

MANATEE

When explorer Christopher Columbus first saw manatees, he thought they were mermaids. He was a bit disappointed that they weren't as beautiful as he thought mermaids would be.

SEA COW? I'M ACTUALLY RELATED TO ELEPHANTS I'LL HAVE YOU KNOW!

Manatees never leave the water, but they have to surface to breathe.

STRANGEOMETER

APPEARANCE		17/25
WEIRD ABILITIES		10/25
? RARITY		14/25
STRANGENESS		15/25
STRANGEOMETER SCORE		56/100

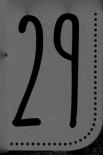

South Pacific Ocean, South Atlantic
Ocean, and Indian Ocean

COME AND SEE ME ON
THE OCEAN BED.

STRANGEOMETER

APPEARANCE		22/25
WEIRD ABILITIES		15/25
RARITY		3/25
STRANGENESS		17/25
STRANGEOMETER SCORE		57/100

SEA PIG

These chubby little fellows are common indeed – but most pe[ople] will never see one, as they live [in] the deepest parts of the ocea[n].

The creatures are a type of sea cucumber and are related to starfish and sea urchins.

Sea pigs have five to seven pairs of feet and get around by walking on the seafloor. They also have feet on their head.

Sea pigs like to hang out in big groups, and when they are in a crowd, they all face in the same direction.

STRANGEOMETER

APPEARANCE		21/25
WEIRD ABILITIES		8/25
RARITY		13/25
STRANGENESS		16/25
STRANGEOMETER SCORE		58/100

HOW ABOUT A SLEEPOVER?

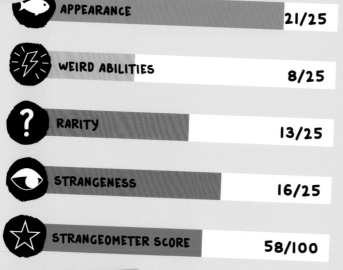

Western, southern, and eastern Australian coasts

STRIPED PYJAMA SQUID

This creature looks like it's dressed ready for bed. Despite its name, it's not really a squid – it's a cuttlefish. Being small and round, it is also often referred to as a striped dumpling squid.

The striped pyjama squid likes to bury itself in sand so only the top of its head is visible. This helps it catch its prey by surprise – boo!

The striped pyjama squid is about 2 in. (5 cm) long and lives in waters that are up to 65 ft. (20 m) deep.

#27

Hawaii, Africa, the Red Sea, southern Japan, the Philippines, and Australia

MY FRIENDS JUST CALL ME HUMUHUMU!

Reef triggerfish use their spines to lock themselves into small cracks in rocks, making it hard for predators to pull them out. When the predator is gone, the triggerfish pulls in its spines and swims off.

REEF TRIGGERFISH

The reef triggerfish is also known by its Hawaiian name, Humuhumunukunukuāpua'a, pronounced who-moo-who-moo-noo-koo-noo-koo-ah-pooah-ah. This means "triggerfish with a snout like a pig."

LONGHORN COWFISH #26

Southern Africa and Indo-Pacific region

The long horns on a cowfish's head make it difficult for predators to swallow the fish. The horns break off easily but can grow back after a few months. The cowfish releases a poisonous chemical when it is scared.

> I HOVER LIKE A SPACESHIP WHEN I SWIM.

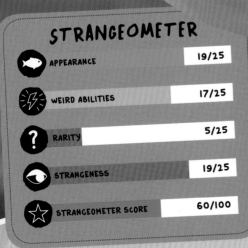

STRANGEOMETER

🐟 APPEARANCE		19/25
⚡ WEIRD ABILITIES		17/25
❓ RARITY		5/25
👁 STRANGENESS		19/25
⭐ STRANGEOMETER SCORE		60/100

Cowfish swim so slowly it's easy to catch them by hand. They blow jets of water at the sand on coral reefs to reveal their prey, and make loud grunts when they're scared.

#25

BLUE WHALE

The blue whale is the biggest creature in the world. In fact, experts think that it is the biggest animal that has ever existed.

I CAN SWIM AT 20 MPH (32 KPH).

The blue whale is also the loudest creature in the world. Its cry can be louder than a jet engine, and scientists think blue whales can hear each other from up to 1,000 mi. (1,600 km) away.

Antarctic, North Pacific, Indian Ocean, North Atlantic

Despite their size, blue whales eat mainly tiny creatures known as krill. But they eat a lot of them – up to 40 million a day.

STRANGEOMETER

🐟	APPEARANCE	17/25
⚡	WEIRD ABILITIES	10/25
❓	RARITY	19/25
👁	STRANGENESS	15/25
⭐	STRANGEOMETER SCORE	61/100

SEA ANGEL

these fairy-like creatures hover in the water, never touching the seabed or coming to the surface.

One type of sea angel oozes a special chemical that predators don't like. A shrimp-like creature called *Hyperiella dilatata* takes advantage of this by kidnapping sea angels and putting them on its back – then it is protected, too!

I'M REALLY A KIND OF SEA SLUG.

Sea angels are tiny and almost completely see-through. they only grow to about 2 in. (5 cm) in length.

STRANGEOMETER

🐟 APPEARANCE		18
⚡ WEIRD ABILITIES		18
❓ RARITY		8
👁 STRANGENESS		18
⭐ STRANGEOMETER SCORE		62

Arctic Ocean and cold waters of the North Pacific and North Atlantic Oceans

Like other octopuses, dumbos can swim by jet propulsion. They shoot out jets of water to push themselves along.

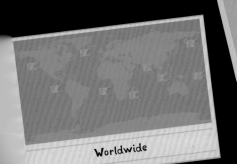

Worldwide

I LIVE DEEPER IN THE OCEAN THAN ANY OTHER OCTOPUS.

The largest dumbo octopus ever recorded was 6 ft. (1.8 m) long and weighed 13 lb. (5.9 kg).

STRANGEOMETER

	APPEARANCE	20/25
	WEIRD ABILITIES	13/25
?	RARITY	10/25
	STRANGENESS	20/25
☆	STRANGEOMETER SCORE	63/100

UMBO CTOPUS

These octopuses were named after the cartoon elephant Dumbo because of the fins that stick out of their heads like big ears. They flap their "ears" to glide through the dark depths where they live – 9,800 ft. (3,000 m) below the surface.

#22

Sloane's viperfish can produce light with their bodies to attract prey.

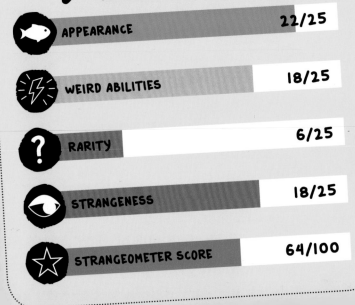

STRANGEOMETER

🐟 APPEARANCE		22/25
⚡ WEIRD ABILITIES		18/25
❓ RARITY		6/25
👁 STRANGENESS		18/25
⭐ STRANGEOMETER SCORE		64/100

The Sloane's viperfish lives at depths of up to 8,200 ft. (2,500 m), so scientists haven't been able to study i...

Tropical and temperate waters

AT NIGHT, I SWIM UP
TO SHALLOWER WATERS
TO FIND MY FOOD.

Although they
look scary,
they are not
dangerous
to humans.

SLOANE'S VIPERFISH

Sloane's viperfish have bigger teeth
compared to the size of their head than
any other fish. Their huge fangs don't
fit inside their closed mouths, so they
curve upward toward their eyes.

Sunflower sea stars have 16 to 24 arms and can be bright orange, yellow, red, brown, or sometimes purple. They have no eyes, brain, or blood, but they have eye-like organs on the tips of their arms.

STRANGEOMETER

APPEARANCE	20/25
WEIRD ABILITIES	18/25
RARITY	5/25
STRANGENESS	22/25
STRANGEOMETER SCORE	65/100

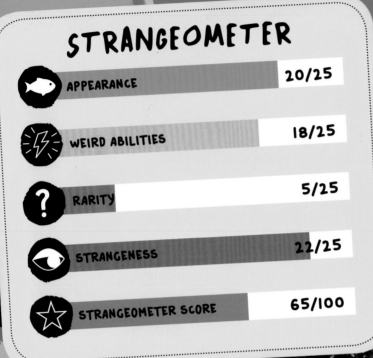

Northeast Pacific

SUNFLOWER SEA STAR

The sunflower sea star is one of the world's largest and fastest-moving starfish. It can travel at 3.3 ft. (1 m) per minute and can grow up to 3.3 ft. (1 m) long.

I CAN SHED AN ARM TO ESCAPE FROM A PREDATOR AND THEN GROW IT BACK.

Like all sea stars, they can push their stomach out through their mouth to catch their prey, so they can eat things that are larger than their mouth.

QUIZ

See if you can answer these questions on the ten ocean beasts you've just learned about!

What is this creature?

4.

1. Where do sea pigs have extra legs?

2. Which animal has fins that look like big ears?

3. What did Christopher Columbus think manatees were?

6. What happens when a longhorn cowfish gets scared?

What is the biggest animal ever to have lived?

7.

8.

5. How do reef triggerfish avoid being eaten?

What is this fish?

10.

9. Which fairy-like creature is actually a sea slug?

How many arms does the sunflower sea star have?

#20

The flamingo tongue snail wraps its brightly patterned soft tissue around the outside of its plain white shell. It can hide its colorful body back inside its shell if it is attacked.

Like all snails, flamingo tongue snails eat with their feet.

FLAMINGO TONGUE SNAIL

These creatures eat poisonous sea fans, but that doesn't bother them – they take the poison and put it in their shell, becoming poisonous themselves.

I LIVE FOR ABOUT TWO YEARS.

Caribbean and South Atlantic coral reefs

STRANGEOMETER

APPEARANCE		22/25
WEIRD ABILITIES		20/25
RARITY		6/25
STRANGENESS		18/25
STRANGEOMETER SCORE		66/100

#19

Some scientists think narwhals use their tusks to determine if nearby icebergs are melting by measuring how salty the water is. Others think the tusks are used as weapons.

You can guess a narwhal's age by its color. Babies are blue-gray and become blue-black, then mottled gray as they get older. By the time they reach old age, narwhals are nearly white.

In the Middle Ages, Vikings used to sell narwhal horns for lots of money to people from more southerly countries, pretending they were unicorn horns.

NARWHAL

Narwhals are a type of whale and live in the cold waters of the Arctic. Their amazing tusks never stop growing – they can reach 9 ft. (3 m) long.

FOLLOW THE TUSK!

STRANGEOMETER

APPEARANCE	24/25
WEIRD ABILITIES	10/25
RARITY	13/25
STRANGENESS	20/25
STRANGEOMETER SCORE	67/100

Arctic waters

#18

CHRISTMAS TREE WORM

These beautiful creatures look like multicolored Christmas trees and live on coral reefs around the world. Once they find a place they like, they burrow into the coral and stay there.

When they are startled, Christmas tree worms quickly pop back inside their burrows.

They have eyes on their gills, which helps them see outside their burrows without having to poke their heads out.

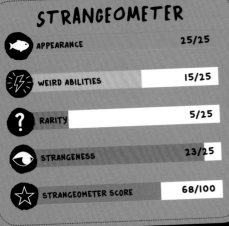

IT'S ALWAYS FESTIVE WHEN WE'RE AROUND!

Pacific and Atlantic Oceans, the Mediterranean Sea, and Australia

DECORATOR CRAB

These creative critters are the fashion designers of the sea. They grab items such as seaweed and corals, and stick them onto their shells as camouflage. Everything stays in place thanks to the hooked hairs that line their shells.

DO YOU LIKE MY NEW LOOK?

Tropical coral reefs

Like other crabs, decorator crabs shed their shells to grow. They often recycle their decorations, carefully removing them from their old shell and sticking them onto their new one.

Some kinds of decorator crab choose ornaments that are poisonous or dangerous, like stinging sea anemones, to protect themselves from predators.

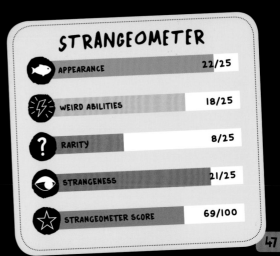

STRANGEOMETER

APPEARANCE	22/25
WEIRD ABILITIES	18/25
RARITY	8/25
STRANGENESS	21/25
STRANGEOMETER SCORE	69/100

#16 PARROTFISH

Parrotfish start off as females and then change into males. As they grow up, they also change color – grown-up parrotfish are brightly colored, but the young are reds, browns, and grays.

MY PARROT-LIKE BEAK HELPS ME NIBBLE CORAL.

If you are walking on a beautiful white sand beach in the Caribbean, you are probably treading on parrotfish poop. Parrotfish eat coral and poop it out as sand!

Shallow tropical and subtropical oceans

STRANGEOMETER

APPEARANCE
20/25

WEIRD ABILITIES
22/25

? RARITY
7/25

STRANGENESS
21/25

★ STRANGEOMETER SCORE
70/100

Parrotfish sleep in
a cocoon made of their
own mucus, which comes from
a strange organ on their heads.
These bizarre sleeping bags
hide them from predators.

Gulf of Mexico, Atlantic, and Southeast Asia

Horseshoe crabs have blue blood, which scientists use to test new drugs. About 1 quart (1 liter) of the blood is worth around $15,000.

STRANGEOMETER

APPEARANCE	23/25
WEIRD ABILITIES	22/25
RARITY	6/25
STRANGENESS	20/25
STRANGEOMETER SCORE	71/100

HORSESHOE CRAB

The horseshoe crab is actually more closely related to spiders than to crabs. While it may not be the most beautiful, it's one of the oldest creatures on Earth.

I'VE LOOKED LIKE THIS FOR 445 MILLION YEARS.

A horseshoe crab has a whopping ten eyes, including one on its tail.

I'M CLOSING A BEACH NEAR YOU SOON.

The Portuguese man-of-war gets its name from the balloon-like part that sits above the water and looks a bit like the sail of a ship. It drifts in the ocean, often in groups of hundreds.

Its tentacles are extremely poisonous and can stretch for 164 ft. (50 m).

STRANGEOMETER

APPEARANCE		22/25
WEIRD ABILITIES		20/25
RARITY		10/25
STRANGENESS		20/25
STRANGEOMETER SCORE		72/100

Atlantic, Pacific, and Indian Oceans

PORTUGUESE MAN-OF-WAR

Often mistaken for a jellyfish, the Portuguese man-of-war is actually a colony of different organisms working together.

HAGFISH

These slippery characters cover themselves with slime to protect themselves from being eaten. A single hagfish can fill a bucket with slime in minutes.

I CAN ABSORB FOOD THROUGH MY SKIN.

Hagfish have four hearts, at least twice as much blood as other fish, and only half a jaw. They also have very floppy skin.

A hagfish can tie itself into a knot.

Pacific and Atlantic Oceans

STRANGEOMETER

APPEARANCE	22/25
WEIRD ABILITIES	22/25
RARITY	6/25
STRANGENESS	23/25
STRANGEOMETER SCORE	73/100

I SUCK UP FOOD THROUGH MY SNOUT. SLURP!

The tail of a male leafy turns bright yellow when he is ready to mate.

STRANGEOMETER

🐟 APPEARANCE	23/25
⚡ WEIRD ABILITIES	13/25
❓ RARITY	20/25
👁 STRANGENESS	18/25
⭐ STRANGEOMETER SCORE	74/100

LEAFY SEADRAGON

To protect themselves from being eaten leafy seadragons have evolved to look like seaweed.

Southern Australia

Female leafies put their bright pink eggs on the males' tails, and the male leafies look after them for a month or so until they hatch.

#11

My spots are unique — just like your fingerprints.

Handfish are a rare kind of anglerfish.

Southern Australia and Tasmania

HANDFISH

Handfish are terrible swimmers. Luckily, they have amazing fins that have developed to look like hands, and they use them to walk across the seafloor.

Fourteen species of handfish have been discovered so far. They grow up to 6 in. (15 cm) long and live in shallow waters off the coasts of Australia and Tasmania.

STRANGEOMETER

APPEARANCE		18/25
WEIRD ABILITIES		17/25
RARITY		21/25
STRANGENESS		19/25
STRANGEOMETER SCORE		75/100

QUIZ

3.

How can you tell a narwhal's age?

What do Christmas tree worms do when startled?

4.

1.

How do flamingo tongue snails eat?

What is this creature?

2.

6.

How do decorator crabs attach things to their shells?

What color is horseshoe crab blood?

7.

8.

5.

Where do parrotfish sleep?

How long are Portuguese man-of-war tentacles?

10.

What is this fish?

9.

What do handfish do with their "hands"?

ANSWERS

1. WITH THEIR FEET. 2. HAGFISH 3. BY ITS COLOR 4. POP BACK INTO THEIR BURROWS 5. IN A COCOON MADE OF THEIR OWN MUCUS 6. WITH HOOKED HAIRS 7. BLUE 8. UP TO 164 FT. (50 M) 9. LEAFY SEADRAGON 10. WALK WITH THEM

#10

One species of pistol shrimp, *Synalpheus pinkfloydi*, is named after the band Pink Floyd because of its pink claw and the huge amount of noise it makes.

STRANGEOMETER

🐟 APPEARANCE		15/25
⚡ WEIRD ABILITIES		25/25
❓ RARITY		11/25
👁 STRANGENESS		25/25
⭐ STRANGEOMETER SCORE		76/100

Worldwide

PISTOL SHRIMP

Also known as snapping shrimp, pistol shrimp fire bubble "bullets" at their enemies. The bubbles reach a speed of 100 mph (160 kph) and make a sound louder than a gunshot.

I'M THE FASTEST GUN IN THE SEA.

For a split second, the shrimp's claw heats the water to a temperature of more than 7,000°F (4,000°C). That's nearly the same temperature as the surface of the sun!

#9

SCIENTISTS ARE STUDYING ME TO HELP FIGHT DISEASE.

Worldwide

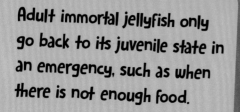

Adult immortal jellyfish only go back to its juvenile state in an emergency, such as when there is not enough food.

IMMORTAL JELLYFISH

This tiny jellyfish can live backwards. It can revert from its adult form back to its juvenile polyp form. This means that if it doesn't get eaten, become ill, or have an accident, it could potentially live forever.

Immortal jellyfish are only 0.2 in. (4.5 mm) long.

STRANGEOMETER

APPEARANCE		17/25
WEIRD ABILITIES		25/25
RARITY		10/25
STRANGENESS		25/25
STRANGEOMETER SCORE		77/100

FIREFLY SQUID

Every firefly squid has tiny light-producing organs all over its body. Between March and June each year, they mass together in seas off the coast of Japan to create amazing blue underwater light shows, like fireworks displays.

No one is quite sure why the squid light up. It could be to speak to each other, to attract a mate, or to scare predators.

The firefly squid is thought to be the only squid that can see in color.

STRANGEOMETER

APPEARANCE		24/25
WEIRD ABILITIES		20/25
RARITY		17/25
STRANGENESS		17/25
STRANGEOMETER SCORE		78/100

Japan

IN JAPAN, WE ARE CAUGHT AND EATEN — AS A 'LIGHT' LUNCH!

STRANGEOMETER

APPEARANCE		20/25
WEIRD ABILITIES		23/25
RARITY		15/25
STRANGENESS		21/25
STRANGEOMETER SCORE		79/100

the shark's body has a natural antifreeze. If you eat its fresh meat, you feel drunk.

MOST OF US ARE ALMOST BLIND BECAUSE OF PARASITES IN OUR EYES.

Sub-Arctic waters

GREENLAND SHARK

This huge shark is the longest-living vertebrate on earth – living for around 400 years. It grows incredibly slowly, at less than 0.4 in. (1 cm) a year.

the Greenland shark is found farther north than any other shark and swims very slowly in the icy waters to save energy.

JAPANESE SPIDER CRAB

The Japanese spider crab measures around 13 ft. (4 m) across. It has eight legs and two long feeding arms, although scientists found that three-quarters of the crabs they studied had lost at least one leg.

> I'M ACTUALLY QUITE A GENTLE CRAB.

STRANGEOMETER

APPEARANCE		24/25
WEIRD ABILITIES		13/25
RARITY		19/25
STRANGENESS		24/25
STRANGEOMETER SCORE		80/100

This crab may look scary, but you're unlikely to meet one – the gigantic beast lives deep in the Pacific Ocean, between 164–2,000 ft. (50–600 m) down.

Japanese spider crabs are the grandfathers of the sea – they are thought to live for around 100 years.

Pacific Ocean

#5 CLOWN FROGFISH

Sometimes known by the less cute name of the warty frogfish, this creature is a master of disguise. Its skin is covered in lots of little bumps and it can match its color to the part of the ocean where it lives.

At about 6 in. (15 cm), it's quite small, but the clown frogfish has a big mouth and can swallow prey as big as itself, which can include other frogfish.

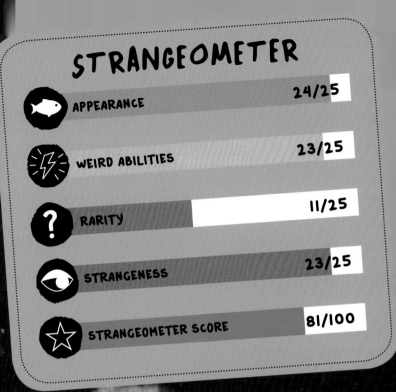

STRANGEOMETER

APPEARANCE		24/25
WEIRD ABILITIES		23/25
RARITY		11/25
STRANGENESS		23/25
STRANGEOMETER SCORE		81/100

Divers love photographing the[m] because they stay s[till] for so long that they[are] easy to snap... if you [can] spot one.

THE SPEED WITH WHICH I CATCH PREY IS ONE OF THE FASTEST IN THE ANIMAL WORLD.

Tropical and subtropical regions of [the] Pacific and Atlantic, as well as th[e] Red Sea and Indian Ocean

#4 RED-LIPPED BATFISH

This pouty-lipped fish definitely has a face you'll never forget. But that's not all – its fins have been specially adapted so that it looks as if it walks on the seabed. It actually can't swim very well.

STRANGEOMETER

APPEARANCE		25/25
WEIRD ABILITIES		20/25
RARITY		17/25
STRANGENESS		20/25
STRANGEOMETER SCORE		82/100

Scientists think that those large, red, kissable lips are designed to attract a mate. They're certainly hard to miss. Mwah!

The batfish also has a long nose that sticks out and is used to attract prey, even if it doesn't attract a mate.

GIVE ME A KISS!

Galapagos Islands

#3 GOBLIN SHARK

The alien-looking goblin shark can slide its jaws forward to catch its prey. Its snout can sense movement, which helps it to zero in on nearby fish.

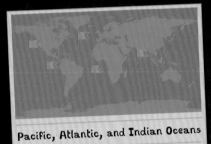

Pacific, Atlantic, and Indian Oceans

I'M SOMETIMES CALLED THE VAMPIRE SHARK BECAUSE I AVOID LIGHT.

Goblin sharks aren't seen often – they live in very deep waters, more than 0.6 miles (1 km) down. Even if you could swim that far down, the shark probably wouldn't see you because its eyesight is very poor.

The goblin shark has been called a "living fossil" because it is related to a family of sharks that were around 125 million years ago.

STRANGEOMETER

APPEARANCE		23/25
WEIRD ABILITIES		17/25
RARITY		23/25
STRANGENESS		20/25
STRANGEOMETER SCORE		83/100

To pretend to be a lionfish, the mimic octopus can change color and shape its eight legs to look like spines.

I WAS ONLY DISCOVERED IN 1998.

MIMIC OCTOPUS

If the ocean had Oscars, the mimic octopus would win them all. If it is being attacked, it can change the way it looks and pretend to be other sea creatures, such as lionfish, sea snakes, starfish, or jellyfish.

STRANGEOMETER

APPEARANCE		21/25
WEIRD ABILITIES		25/25
RARITY		14/25
STRANGENESS		25/25
STRANGEOMETER SCORE		85/100

Scientists have discovered 15 different disguises of the octopus, including the squid.

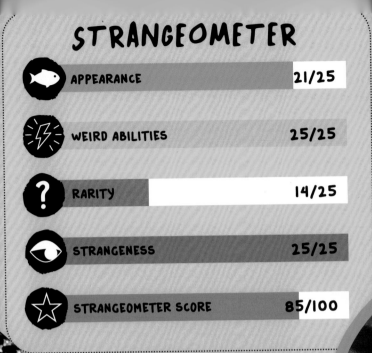

Indo-Pacific region

To look like a scary sea snake, the master of disguise hides in a hole and pokes out two of its legs, which it places in opposite directions.

#1

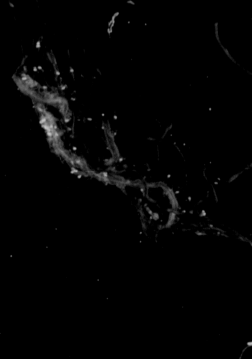

SOME OF US CAN GROW UP TO 3.3 FT. (1 M) IN LENGTH. DON'T HAVE NIGHTMARES!

A piece of the female anglerfish's spine hangs over her head, like a fishing pole with a tasty worm attached. The tip of the pole glows in the dark to attract smaller prey and lure them into the anglerfish's mouth.

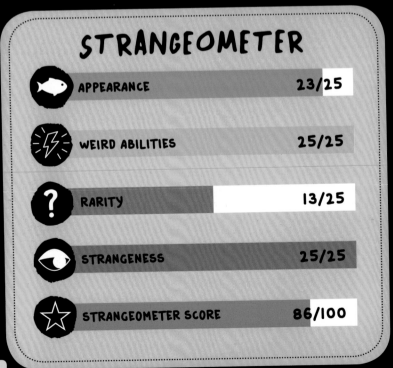

STRANGEOMETER

🐟 APPEARANCE	23/25
⚡ WEIRD ABILITIES	25/25
❓ RARITY	13/25
👁 STRANGENESS	25/25
⭐ STRANGEOMETER SCORE	86/100

ANGLERFISH

this creepy-looking creature mostly lives at the bottom of the deep, dark Atlantic and Antarctic Oceans, and it has some super-weird habits.

Atlantic and Antarctic Oceans

Male anglerfish are much smaller than females. When they find a female, they grab onto her with their sharp teeth and stick to her, losing their eyes and most of their internal organs. Females can carry six or more males on their bodies.

QUIZ

See if you can answer these questions on the ten ocean beasts you've just learned about!

3. Why are many Greenland sharks almost blind?

What is thought to be the only squid that can see in color?

1. What temperature does the pistol shrimp's claw snap produce?

4.

2. What is this creature?

6.

Why is it easy to take a picture of a clown frogfish?

7.

What is this fish?

5.

How big is the Japanese spider crab?

8.

What is the goblin shark's nickname?

9.

What does the female angler fish use to attract food?

10.

How many disguises does the mimic octopus have?

GLOSSARY

algae	very small organisms (living things) that look like plants and grow in or near water
colony	a group of animals of the same type living or growing together
coral	a marine animal that stays in one place undersea and forms a hard rock-like substance
fang	a large pointed tooth
fossil	the remains of an animal or plant preserved in rock for millions of years
gill	the body part of a fish or other marine creature, which it uses to breathe
mammal	warm-blooded animals that breathe air; the females have glands that produce milk for their young
Middle Ages	the period of history between about 500 and 1500 AD
mollusk	an animal with no spine and a soft body, often covered in a shell
mucus	the slimy liquid that is produced by the nose
organ	a part of the body
organism	a living thing
parasite	an organism that lives on and feeds off another organism
plankton	really, really small plants and animals that float in the sea
polyp	a simple tube-shaped water organism
predator	an animal that hunts and eats other another animals
prey	an animal that is hunted and eaten by other animals
quill pen	a pen made from the feather of a goose or other bird, used in the past
species	a type of animal or plant with similar characteristics
subtropical	the areas that are immediately north or south of the tropics (see tropical)
temperate	a temperature that is neither very hot nor very cold
tentacle	a long thin arm-like part of an animal's body used for catching food, moving around, or defense
tropical	relating to the tropics, which is the area on either side of the equator, the imaginary line around the center of the Earth
vertebrate	a creature with a spine